PIANO | VOCAL | GUITAR

CONTEMPORARY COFFEEHOUSE
- S O N G S -

ISBN 978-1-5400-3921-7

 **HAL•LEONARD®**

Visit Hal Leonard Online at
www.halleonard.com

Contact us:
Hal Leonard
7777 West Bluemound Road
Milwaukee, WI 53213
Email: info@halleonard.com

In Europe, contact:
Hal Leonard Europe Limited
42 Wigmore Street
Marylebone, London, W1U 2RN
Email: info@halleonardeurope.com

In Australia, contact:
Hal Leonard Australia Pty. Ltd.
4 Lentara Court
Cheltenham, Victoria, 3192 Australia
Email: info@halleonard.com.au

CONTENTS

ALL I WANT
from the Motion Picture Soundtrack THE FAULT IN OUR STARS

Words and Music by JAMES FLANNIGAN,
STEPHEN GARRIGAN, MARK PRENDERGAST
and VINCENT MAY

With a lilt, in one

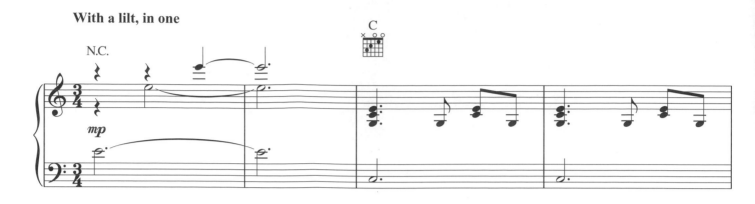

BABYLON

Words and Music by
DAVID GRAY

BANANA PANCAKES

Words and Music by
JACK JOHNSON

BUDAPEST

Words and Music by GEORGE BARNETT
and JOEL POTT

BLACK HORSE
AND THE CHERRY TREE

Words and Music by
KATIE TUNSTALL

Moderately, with a beat

Woo, hoo, _____ woo, hoo, _____ woo,

hoo, _____ woo, hoo. Well, my

heart knows me bet-ter than I know my-self _____ so I'm _____ gon-na let it do all the talk - in'. Woo,

CHASING CARS

Words and Music by GARY LIGHTBODY,
TOM SIMPSON, PAUL WILSON,
JONATHAN QUINN and NATHAN CONNOLLY

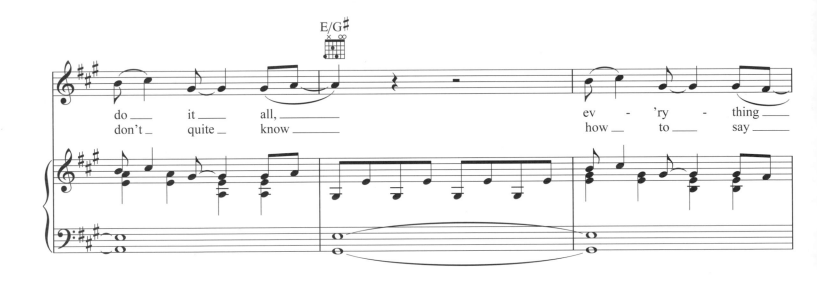

FALLIN' FOR YOU

Words and Music by COLBIE CAILLAT
and RICK NOWELS

50

COME ON GET HIGHER

Words and Music by MATT NATHANSON
and MARK WEINBERG

CONSTANT CRAVING

Words and Music by K.D. Lang
and BEN MINK

Brightly, with a beat

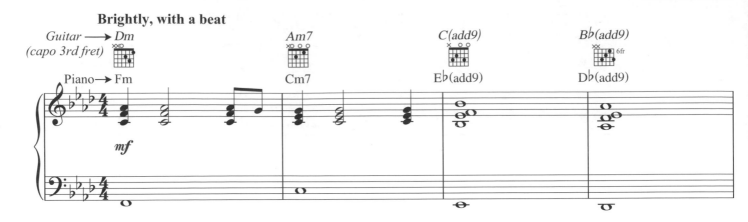

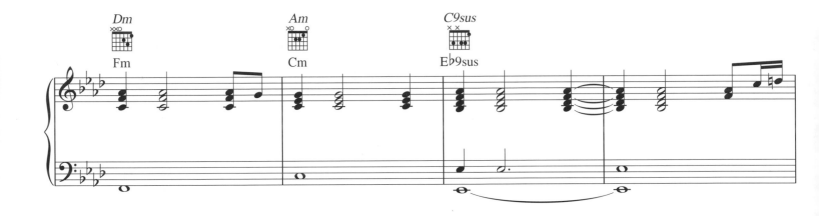

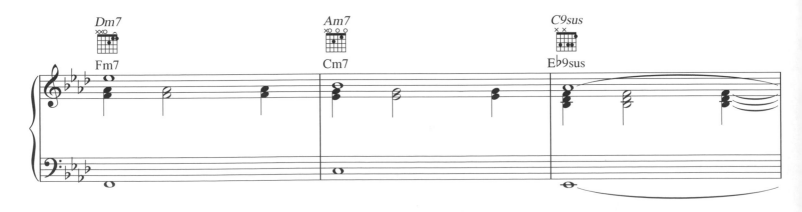

DON'T KNOW WHY

Words and Music by
JESSE HARRIS

FIRST DAY OF MY LIFE

Words and Music by
CONOR OBERST

74

FAST CAR

Words and Music by
TRACY CHAPMAN

HALLELUJAH

Words and Music by
LEONARD COHEN

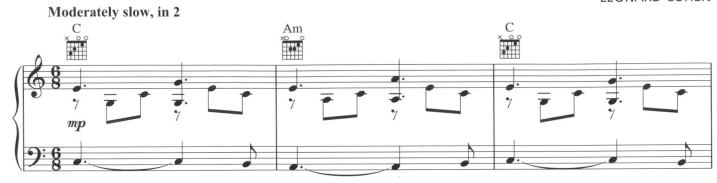

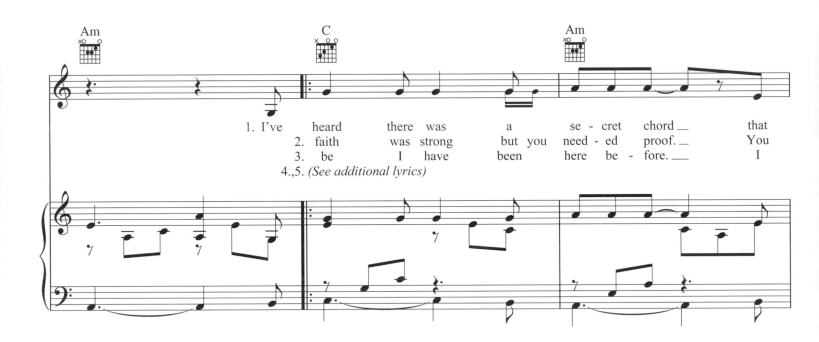

1. I've heard there was a se-cret chord ___ that
2. faith was strong but you need-ed proof. ___ You
3. be I have been here be-fore. ___ I
4.,5. (See additional lyrics)

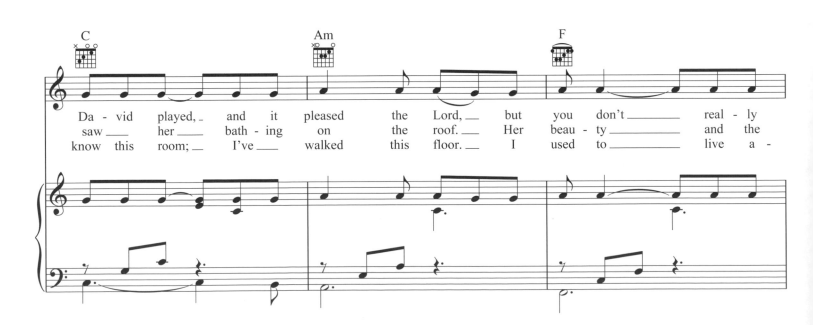

Da-vid played, ___ and it pleased the Lord, ___ but you don't ___ real-ly
saw ___ her ___ bath-ing on the roof. ___ Her beau-ty ___ and the
know this room; ___ I've ___ walked this floor. ___ I used to ___ live a-

care for mu - sic, ___ do you? ___ It
moon - light o - ver - threw you. ___ She
lone be - fore I ___ knew you. ___ I've

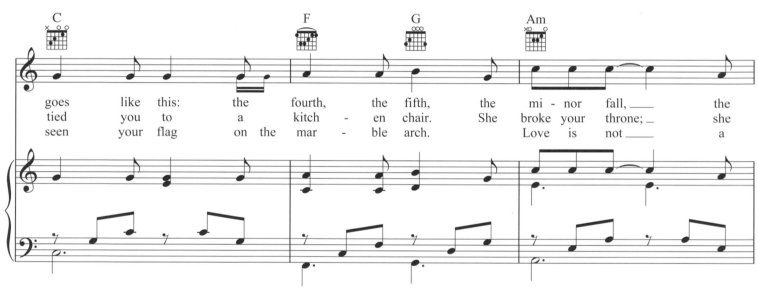

goes like this: the fourth, the fifth, the mi - nor fall, ___ the
tied you to a kitch - en chair. She broke your throne; ___ she
seen your flag on the mar - ble arch. Love is not ___ a

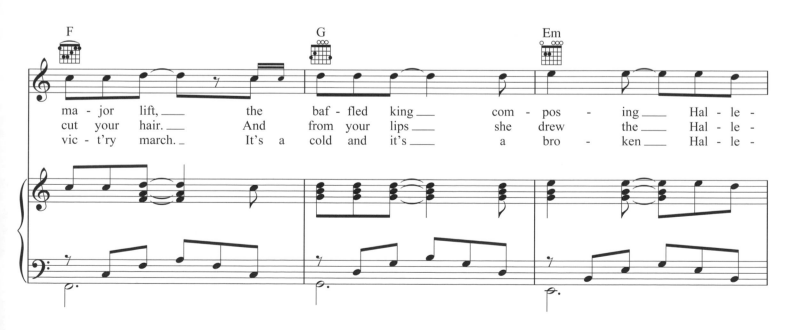

ma - jor lift, ___ the baf - fled king ___ com - pos - ing ___ Hal - le -
cut your hair. ___ And from your lips ___ she drew the ___ Hal - le -
vic - t'ry march. ___ It's a cold and it's ___ a bro - ken ___ Hal - le -

Am   F

lu - jah._____ Hal - le - lu - jah._____ Hal - le -

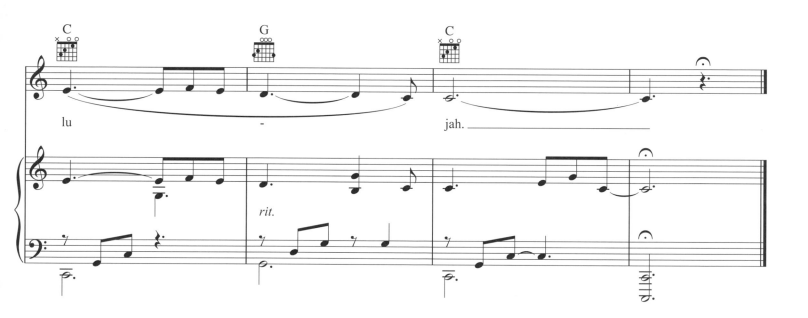

C   G   C

lu   -   jah._____

rit.

Additional Lyrics

4. There was a time you let me know
What's real and going on below.
But now you never show it to me, do you?
And remember when I moved in you.
The holy dark was movin', too,
And every breath we drew was Hallelujah.
Chorus

5. Maybe there's a God above,
And all I ever learned from love
Was how to shoot at someone who outdrew you.
And it's not a cry you can hear at night.
It's not somebody who's seen the light.
It's a cold and it's a broken Hallelujah.
Chorus

HAVE IT ALL

Words and Music by JASON MRAZ,
JACOB KASHER HINDLIN and DAVID HODGES

IF IT MAKES YOU HAPPY

Words and Music by JEFF TROTT
and SHERYL CROW

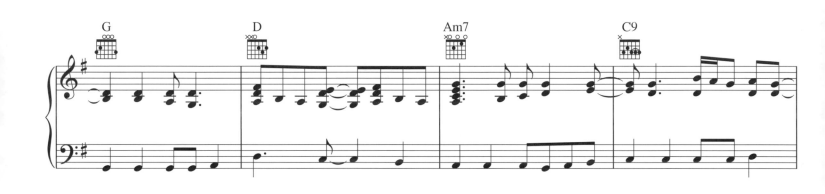

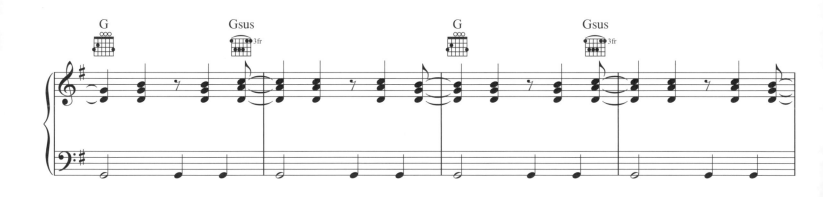

I WILL FOLLOW YOU INTO THE DARK

Words and Music by
BENJAMIN GIBBARD

ICE CREAM

Words and Music by
SARAH McLACHLAN

Your love is bet-ter than ice ____ cream,
Your love is bet-ter than choc - 'late,

Vocal written one octave higher than sung.

IF WE WERE VAMPIRES

Words and Music by
MICHAEL ISBELL

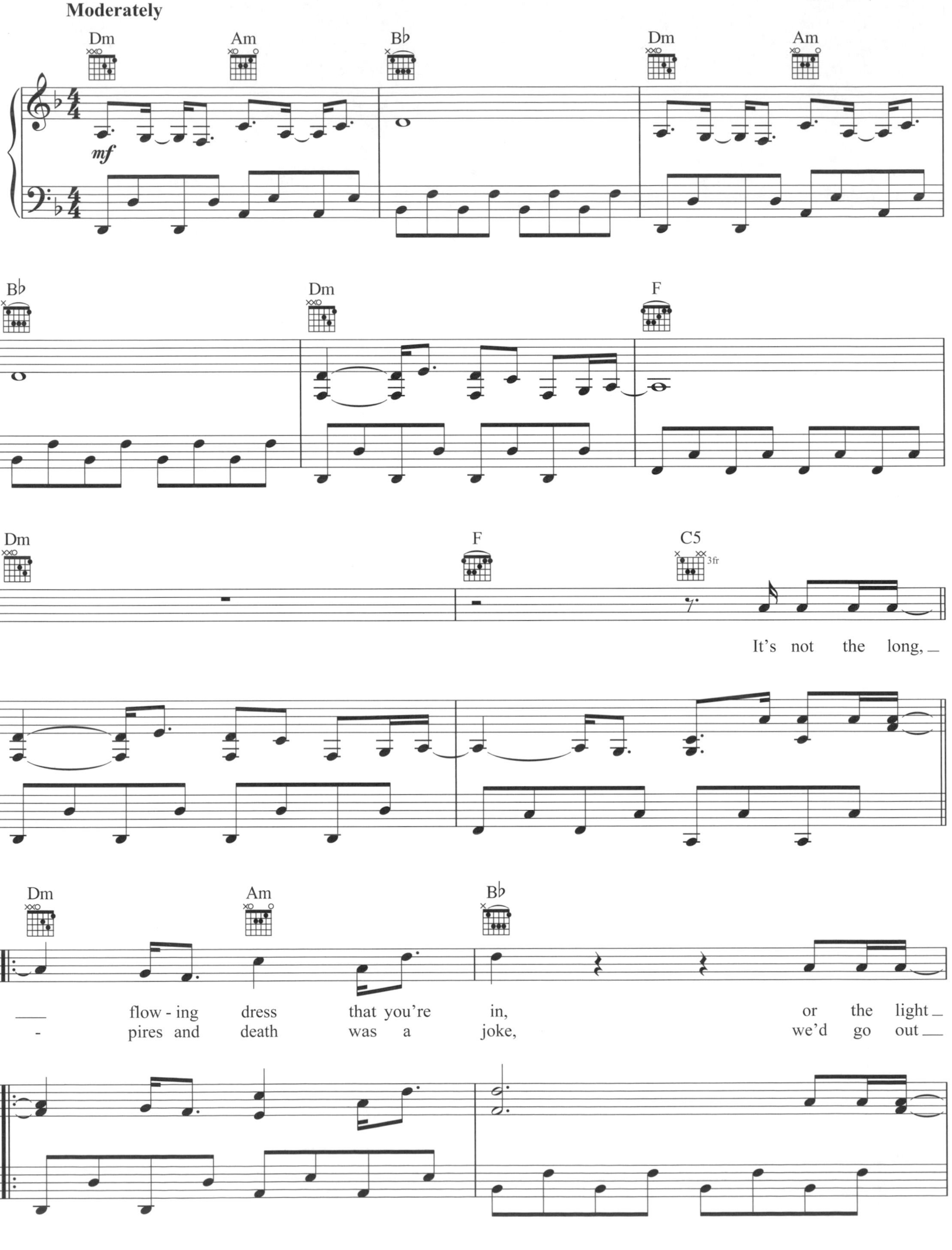

Moderately
Dm
Am
B♭
Dm
Am
mf
B♭
Dm
F
Dm
F
C5
3fr
It's not the long, _
Dm
Am
B♭
_ flow - ing dress that you're in, or the light _
- pires and death was a joke, we'd go out _

know-ing that ___ this can't ___ go on ___ for - ev - er.

LEAST COMPLICATED

Words and Music by
EMILY SALIERS

125

LET HIM FLY

Words and Music by
PATTY GRIFFIN

Moderately, with feeling

Ain't no talk-in' to this man.

Ain't no pret-ty oth-er side. _____ Ain't no way

130

LET IT GO

Words and Music by JAMES BAY
and PAUL BARRY

* Recorded a half step higher.

LOST BOY

Words and Music by
RUTH BERHE

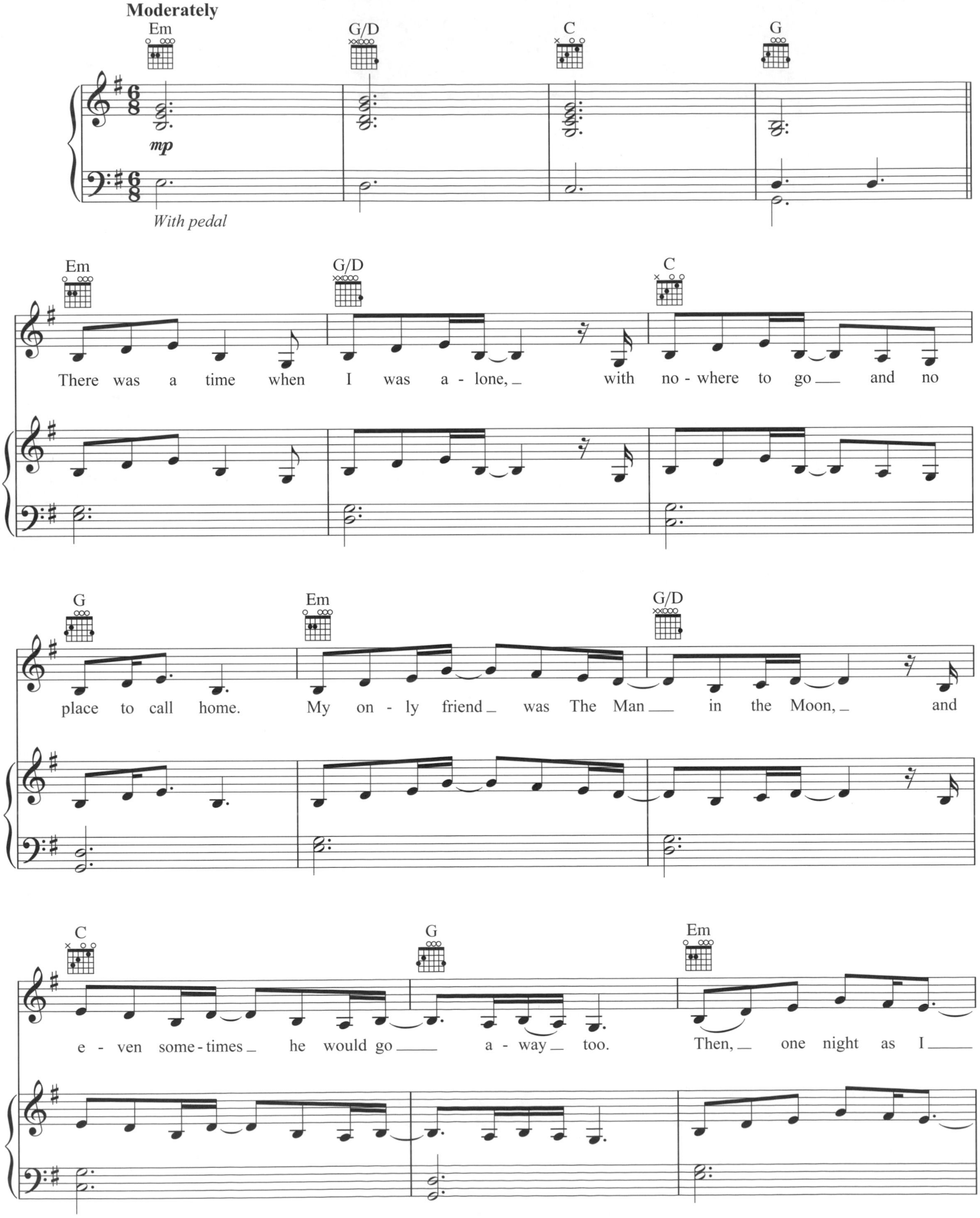

Moderately
Em G/D C G
mp
With pedal
Em G/D C
There was a time when I was a - lone, with no - where to go and no
G Em G/D
place to call home. My on - ly friend was The Man in the Moon, and
C G Em
e - ven some - times he would go a - way too. Then, one night as I

LUCKY

Words and Music by JASON MRAZ,
COLBIE CAILLAT and TIMOTHY FAGAN

Female vocal sung one octave lower than written.

*Substitute half rest on D.S.

THE NIGHT WE MET

Words and Music by
BEN SCHNEIDER

MEET VIRGINIA

Words and Music by PAT MONAHAN,
JAMES STAFFORD, ROBERT HOTCHKISS,
CHARLES COLIN and SCOTT UNDERWOOD

No, ___ no. ___
(Vocal 1st time only)

No, ___ no. ___

No, ___ no. ___

She on - ly ___ drinks cof - fee ___ at mid - night when the
You see, ___ her con - fi - dence is trag - ic, when but her

ONE OF US

Words and Music by
ERIC BAZILIAN

If   God had   a   name, __
God had   a   face, __

PUT YOUR RECORDS ON

Words and Music by JOHN BECK,
STEVEN CHRISANTHOU and CORINNE BAILEY RAE

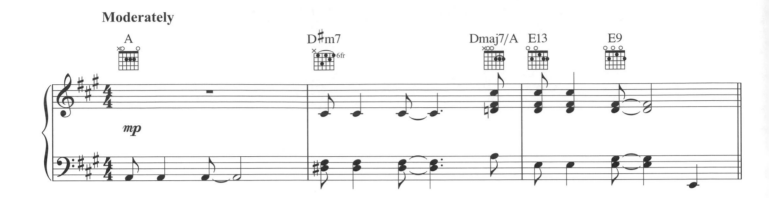

Three ___ lit - tle birds sat on my win - dow
Blue ___ as the sky, sun - burnt and lone - ly,

and they told me I don't need to wor - ry.
sip - pin' tea in a bar by the road - side. ___

SAVE TONIGHT

Words and Music by
EAGLE EYE CHERRY

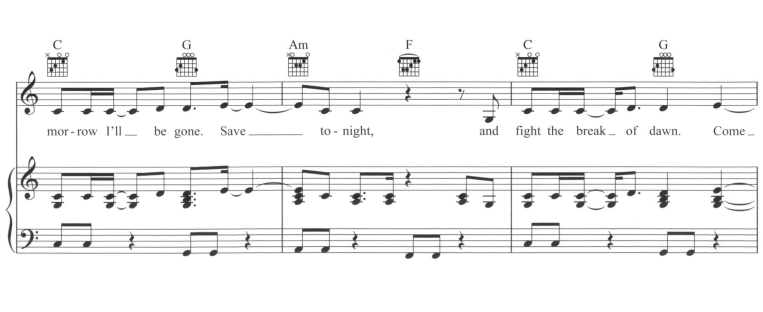

RIVER

Words and Music by TODD MICHAEL BRIDGES,
CHRIS VIVION, JOSHUA BLOCK
and AUSTIN JENKINS

Gentle Folk Ballad

Been trav-'ling these wide _ roads _ for so _ long. _ My heart's been

far _ from You, _ ten thou-sand _ miles _ gone. _

ROUND HERE

Words and Music by ADAM DURITZ, DAVID BRYSON,
CHARLES GILLINGHAM, MATTHEW MALLEY, STEVE BOWMAN,
CHRISTOPHER ROLDAN, DAVID JANUSKO and DAN JEWETT

SAY YOU WON'T LET GO

Words and Music by STEVEN SOLOMON,
JAMES ARTHUR and NEIL ORMANDY

Moderate Ballad

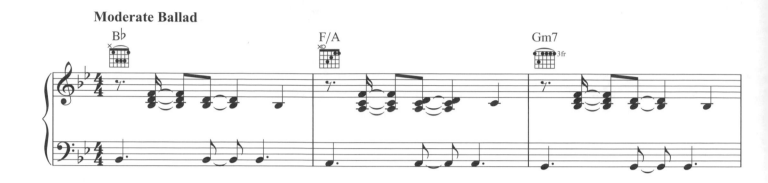

I met you in the dark, you lit me up,
I wake you up with some break-fast in bed,

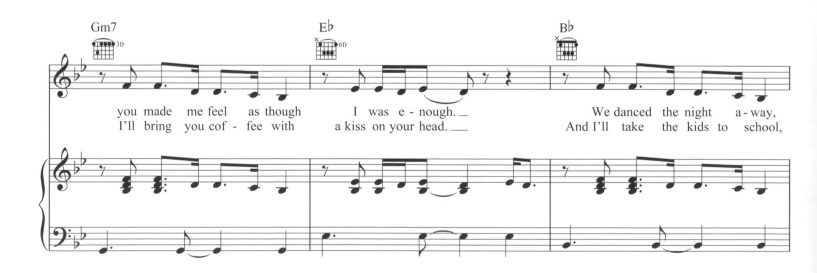

you made me feel as though I was e-nough. _
I'll bring you cof-fee with a kiss on your head. _
We danced the night a-way,
And I'll take the kids to school,

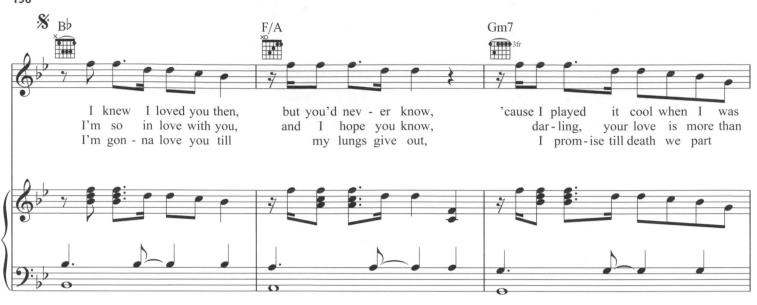

I knew I loved you then, but you'd nev-er know, 'cause I played it cool when I was
I'm so in love with you, and I hope you know, dar-ling, your love is more than
I'm gon-na love you till my lungs give out, I prom-ise till death we part

scared of let-ting go. _____ I know I need-ed you, but I nev-er showed,
worth its weight in gold. _____ We've come so far, my dear, look how we've grown,
like in our vows. _____ So I wrote this song for you, now ev-'ry-bod-y knows

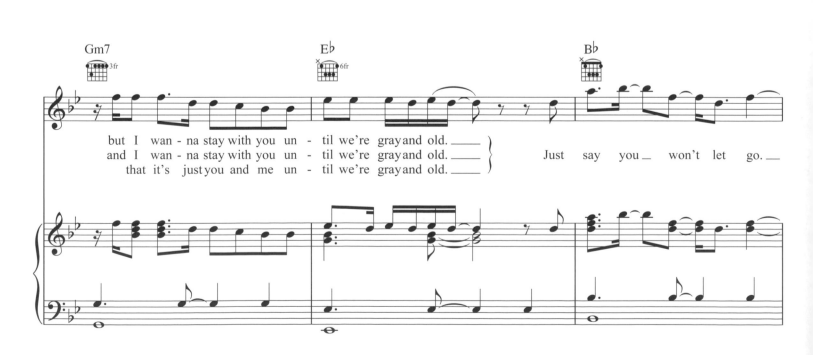

but I wan-na stay with you un - til we're gray and old. _____ }
and I wan-na stay with you un - til we're gray and old. _____ } Just say you_ won't let go.
that it's just you and me un - til we're gray and old. _____ }

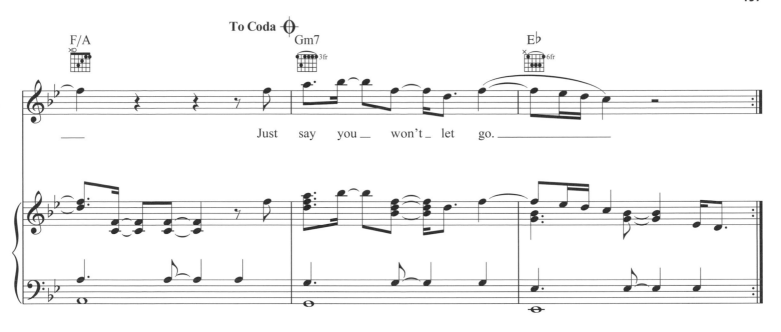

Just say you __ won't __ let go. _____

I wan - na live with you __ e - ven when we're ghosts, __

'cause you were al - ways there for me when I need - ed you most. _____

THIS TOWN

Words and Music by NIALL HORAN,
MICHAEL NEEDLE, DANIEL BRYER,
and JAMIE SCOTT

If the / 'Cause if the whole world _ was watch - ing, _ I'd

still dance _ with you; drive high - ways _ and by - ways _ to

be there _ with you. O - ver _ and o - ver, _ the

on - ly _ truth: ev - 'ry - thing _ comes back _

6TH AVENUE HEARTACHE

Words and Music by
JAKOB DYLAN

208

SIMPLE SONG

Words and Music by
MICHAEL ROSENBERG

Moderately, in 2

SKINNY LOVE

Words and Music by
JUSTIN VERNON

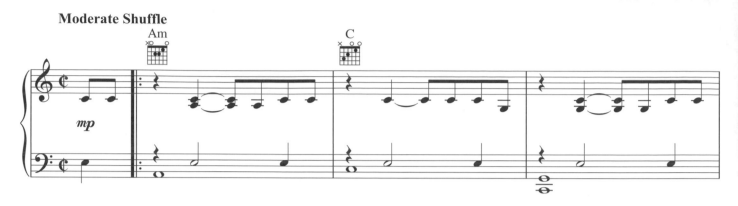

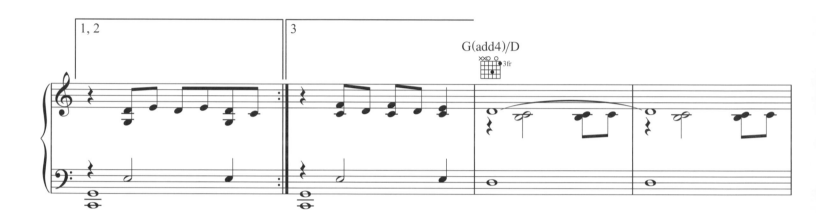

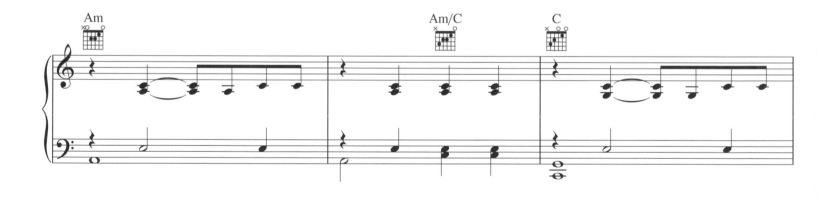

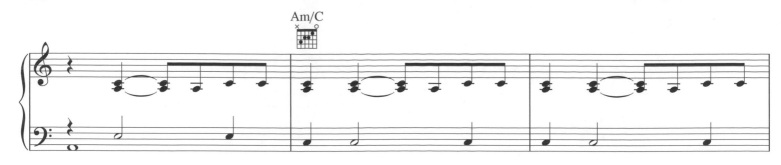

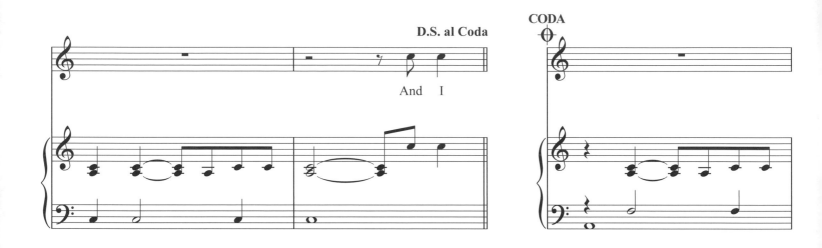

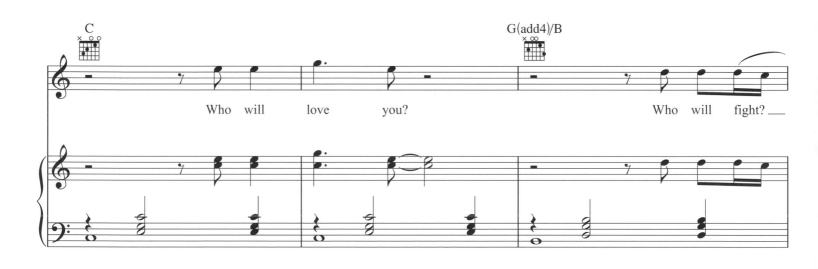

far be - hind?

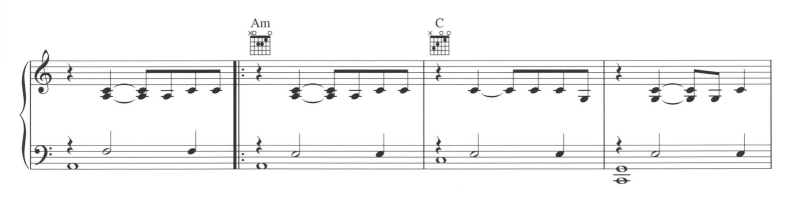

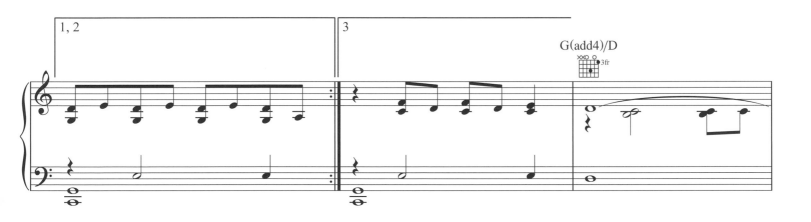

STAY

Words and Music by
LISA LOEB

* Recorded a half step higher.

STEAL MY KISSES

Words and Music by
BEN HARPER

Moderate groove

mf detached

I pulled in to Nash - ville, Ten - nes - see, but

you would - n't e - ven come_ a - round_ to see me. And

al - ways have __ to steal __ my kiss - es from _____ you. _____

SUCH A SIMPLE THING

Words and Music by
RAY LAMONTAGNE

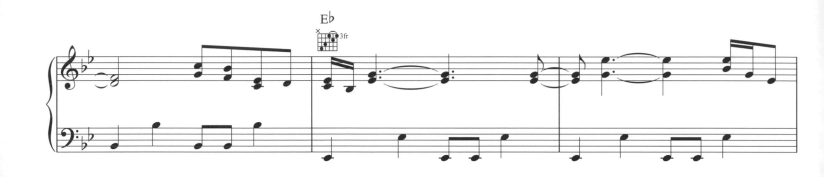

Tell me what your heart wants,

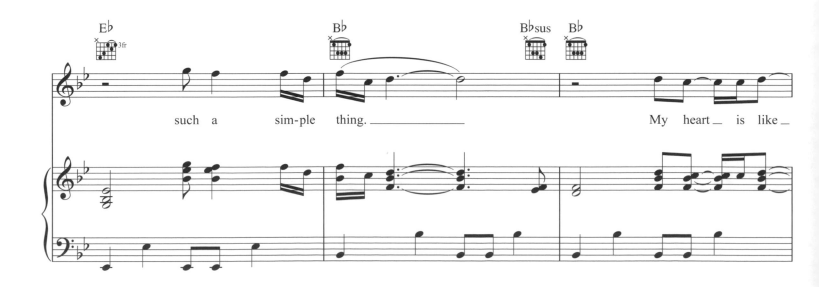

such a sim-ple thing. _____ My heart __ is like __

SUNNY CAME HOME

Words and Music by SHAWN COLVIN
and JOHN LEVENTHAL

Sun-ny came home to her fa-v'rite room. _ Sun-ny sat down in the

SWEET CREATURE

Words and Music by HARRY STYLES
and THOMAS HULL

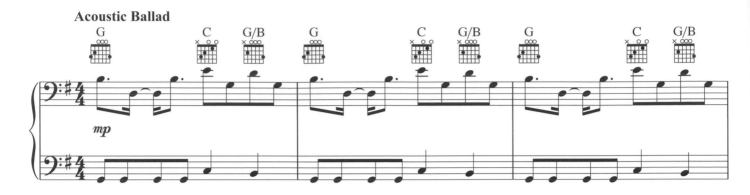

Acoustic Ballad

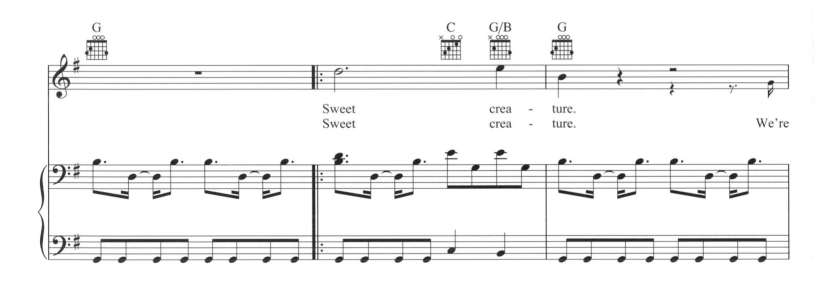

Sweet   crea - ture.
Sweet   crea - ture.   We're

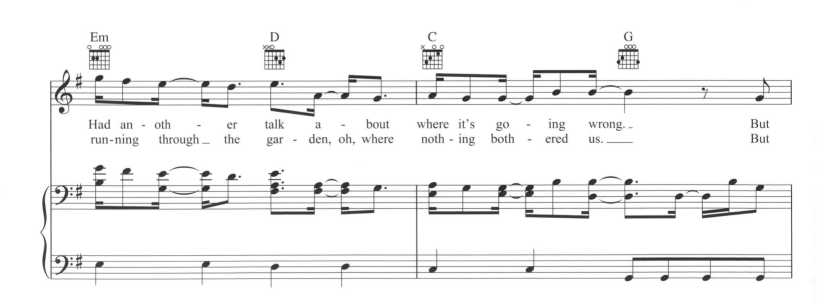

Had an - oth - er talk a - bout where it's go - ing wrong.___ But
run - ning through___ the gar - den, oh, where noth - ing both - ered us. ___ But

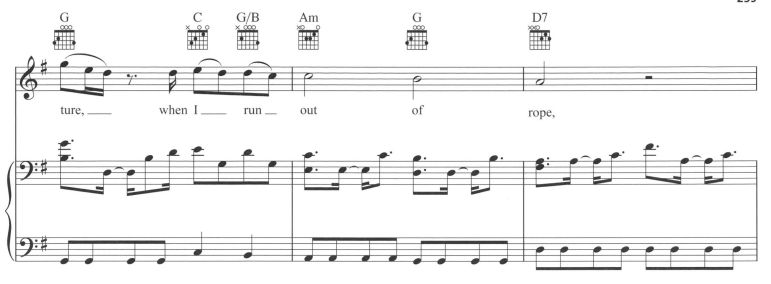

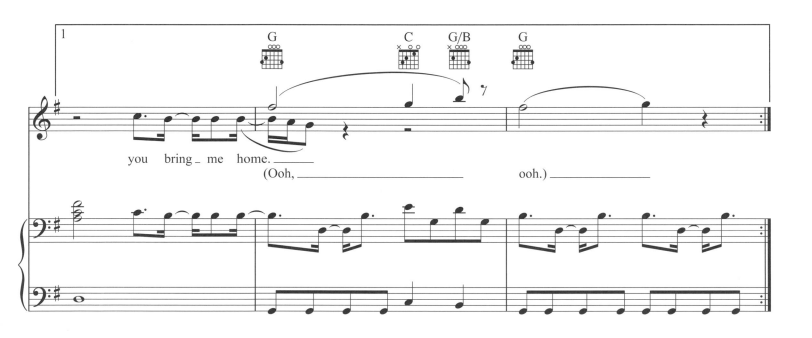

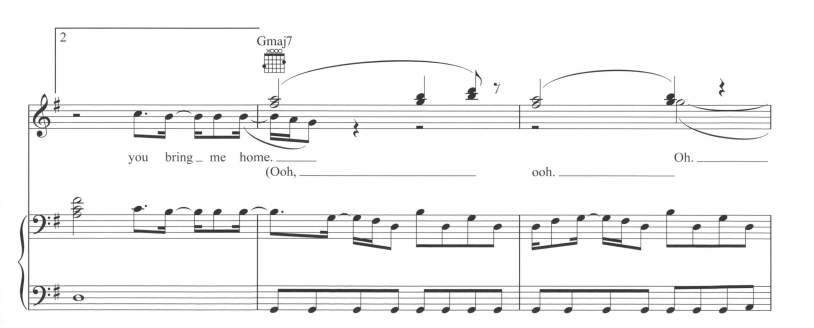

TROUBLE

Words and Music by
RAY LaMONTAGNE

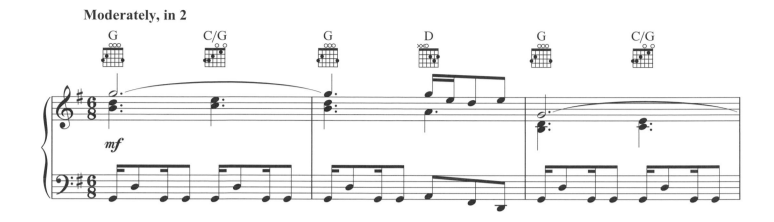

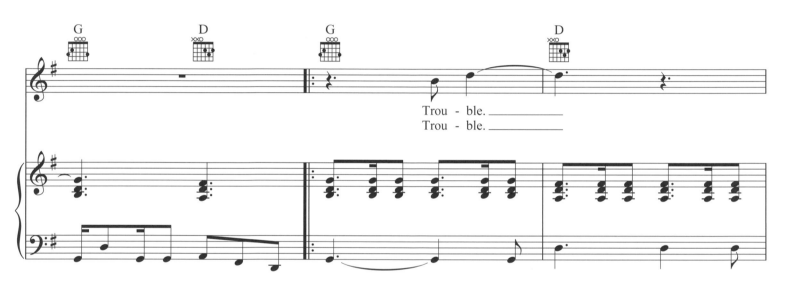

Trou - ble. _____
Trou - ble. _____

Trou - ble, trou - ble, trou - ble, trou - ble.   Trou - ble   been
Trou - ble, trou - ble, trou - ble, trou - ble.   Feels like   ev - 'ry

264

TOM'S DINER

Music and Lyrics by
SUZANNE VEGA

TORN

Words and Music by PHIL THORNALLEY,
SCOTT CUTLER and ANNE PREVIN

Moderate Rock

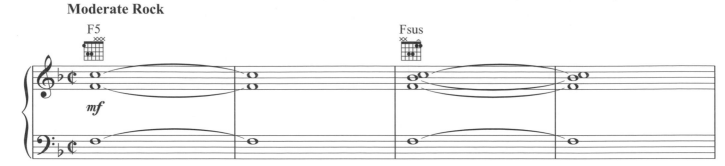

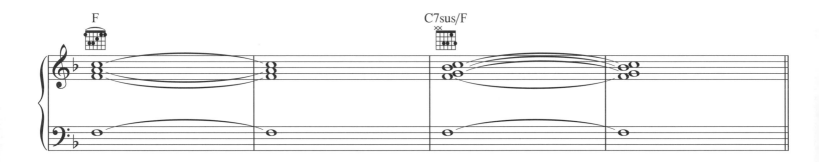

I thought I saw ____ a man ____ brought ____
Well, you could-n't be ____ that man ____ I
So, I guess ____ the for-tune tell-

____ to life.
____ a-dored. ____
-er's right. ____

He was warm,
You don't seem to know
I should-'ve seen

THE WAY I AM

Words and Music by
INGRID MICHAELSON

*Chords implied by bass (next 20 bars).

If you ___ were fall - ing, ___ then I ___ would

catch you. ___ You need ___ a light, ___

I'd find a match. ___ 'Cause I ___
(I ___

WONDERWALL

Words and Music by
NOEL GALLAGHER

To-day is gon-na be the day that they're

gon-na throw it back to you. __ By now you should-'ve some-how re-al-

ised what you got-ta do. __ I don't be-lieve __ that an-y-bod-y

WHAT I AM

Words and Music by BRANDON ALY,
EDIE BRICKELL, JOHN BUSH,
JOHN HOUSER and KENNETH WITHROW

WHO WILL SAVE YOUR SOUL

Words and Music by
JEWEL MURRAY

*Originally sung an octave lower.

YOU LEARN

Lyrics by ALANIS MORISSETTE
Music by ALANIS MORISSETTE and GLEN BALLARD

I _____ rec-om-mend get-ting your heart tram-pled on to
I _____ rec-om-mend bit-ing off more than you can chew to

an-y-one,   yeah. _____
an-y-one,   I _____ cer-tain-ly do.